The Secret Side of Dorset Street

poems by

Eileen M Brunetto

Finishing Line Press
Georgetown, Kentucky

The Secret Side
of Dorset Street

ACKNOWLEDGMENTS

Members of the Addison County Writers' Group for their encouragement and
generous critique of my work during online pandemic days.

Zig Zag literary magazine for publishing my poems, "The Problem with Leaving
a Light On," "Heart and Bone," and "Voice of the Falls," in recent issues; and for
featuring my work and profile in Issue 15, Fall 2023.

Special thanks to the Poetry Society of Vermont for inviting me to serve on their
poetry magazine's *The Mountain Troubadour* editorial board.

Deep gratitude to my husband, Charles, and my children, for their love and support
along the way.

Publisher: Leah Huete de Maines
Editor: Christen Kincaid
Cover Art: Eileen M. Brunetto
Author Photo: Charles Brunetto
Cover Design: Elizabeth Maines McCleavy

Order online: www.finishinglinepress.com
also available on amazon.com

Author inquiries and mail orders:
Finishing Line Press
PO Box 1626
Georgetown, Kentucky 40324
USA

Contents

The Problem with Leaving a Light On..1

Heart and Bone...2

Table Flowers...3

Nutrients...4

Green Man...6

Listening to Spanish Music at Night..7

Random 8

Winter's Work...9

It's All Happening at Once 10

Worry..12

Tiny Plants..13

Moon Thief...14

The Secret Side of Dorset Street...15

People Watching..16

The Scent of Hay...17

Evening Call...18

Black..19

Night Walk 20

Long Life Rant...22

Garden People..23

Wild Bird 24

Voice of the Falls...25

Recycled Earth...26

Day Sense..27

Through a Train Window...29

Spring Thaw..30

Jung's Coffee Cup 31

Saving...32

While We Wait..34

The Opening..35

The Problem with Leaving a Light On

you have left the light on again
without meaning to
then the cat jumps up
this allure of unconditional affection

tonight, his silky purr
presents as an offer of comfort;
or perhaps the animal wishes
to take something from you instead,
the thing you hold close

he stretches across your flattened, resting body
one paw on your heart
the other feels for your jugular, your blood
you can never be sure

Heart and Bone

she never made fancy efforts toward
self-care

nylon stockings bought at Woolworth's
secured the 1960's way with a garter
fire engine red lipstick
a one-woman one-stop American girl beauty show

I never once saw her nails painted
which is why the Revlon essential beige
she wore at her own funeral, seemed so remarkable
(me, by sheer coincidence, wearing the same color to offset my
black dress)

her freckled hands, now bruised
hands that had picked flowers, changed
diapers, baked legendary crumb cake,
wrote thank you notes, managed money, waved goodbye...

lovingly stroked my little brother's
dying chameleon
cooed softly
as she cradled its limp body

if only the funeral attendant could have
allowed me that one small task
to have held her soft fingers,
the tips of them rested against mine.

anointed the beige in gentle brushstrokes
I don't even know if the rules allow
outsiders to take on such a job
I could have at least asked

the note I wrote her, our last secret,
placed inside the casket

I wish I had tucked it in her hand,
wrapped her polished thumb and
forefinger around the words
nails painted neutral, same as the way she played life

fair, straightforward, truthful
color of flesh and bone
heart and soul

Table Flowers

Yes, we'll sell it, I promised him.
this walnut, odd-shaped table
has lived out its time with us

no longer practical,
nor the object of
beauty and efficiency I once admired
up-cycled by the vintage shop matron
I had been naively impressed

now I doubt I'll be able to
give it away
and if I give it away,
the new owner will sell it

that's where my stinginess
separates me from the saints
someone will make money
from my money

I don't know why we can't agree
hasn't this table served us well?
we fashioned it into the perfect wine bar
for your big birthday

the party where every friend
came to toast, pay homage

a little boy sang.
a cake so delicious
guests gushed
we all had a moment

and the table was there like family
our witness,
holding up sparkling wine glasses
a crystal vase filled with asters and mums
brought by a guest

Nutrients

nourishment of body and soul
the concern amplifies
each time I drive past
Dandelion Farm

this past summer
more than ever before
in dreams I ask,
will the farmers be here next growing season?

will license to grow become government requisite
and how much
will it cost the farmer?

indeed, what will it cost you and me
to grow our own tomatoes and beans
in dollars and freedom
in our own backyards

or will the beans all live on a shelf at Whole Foods until shopping day?
don't worry,
they'll be waiting for you
they've got staying power like you wouldn't believe

boxes of cereal
in an Amazon cart
so cheap when you order in bulk
buy, click, stock up
~~~~~
we now have the egg
which has taken on gourmet status
"they're still a good deal
come on, it's such quality protein"
how many ways can you prepare an egg,
get creative

they've been weirdly sneaking them onto your burger for years
advancing their status in the
hierarchy of foods
while we weren't paying attention

eggs
innocent origins
babies
fields of grain
a cup of water
you'll remember the crust of bread

Green Man

I miss the woods and hillside
iris and waving grass
rare red stone in the shape of a heart

and this kitchen window
where I gaze upon my morning
of mist and birdsong
sip coffee as you sleep

today, there's a box
I've not seen it before
filled with tree limbs and branches
a blanket of high-summer leaves.
form beneath

shhhh, I tell myself
surely, he will go away

made of skin and bones and eyes
this lost being
brushes off the green.
requests admittance

I offer eggs and toast
whisper, he may not come in

another morning dream
fades in and away
more real,
more terrifying than nighttime
than nature

I send you telepathic messages
please, please wake up

Listening to Spanish Music at Night

I keep thinking lately
about the year I turned 15
and how I was so hung up
on that lake

the one where
when I was younger,
went fishing with a stick
some string and a ball of bread
out to prove to myself
I could catch a sunnie on my own

remove it from the hook
and throw it back into
gray-green water
a quiet violent way to establish independence

cold moon
the lake at night
little fires along its banks
where skater friends were up to my kind of trouble without me

me inside the homes of wealthy townspeople
babysitting for kids,
asleep when I arrived
as if they had been drugged.

it would have made more sense to feel productive
earn my keep
tell them a bedtime story
but I never even saw their faces

instead, I chose the lake's sheen
watched flames smolder
watched late night movies

now I'm far away from that lake
and what I do for fun is so unlike
fishing for sunnies
or flirting with boys by fires

I walk and read
try to help where I can
try to sleep
listen to Spanish guitar playing in the dark

Random

sometimes I pray on behalf of random strangers and acquaintances

I don't think everyone will understand this

I bow my head and darn if
plain words don't turn into
an involuntary pinpointed ask

golden warmth radiates
like sun over my shoulder
fills my fingertips
it's a little embarrassing to admit

as a rule, I don't
say formal Hail Marys,
so regimented and passé,
but there they are, regardless.
a habit that hasn't died off
along with the rest of my old religion

now I'm anti-religion
it's more about supplication and acceptance
distribution of good intentions
a form of free-form cure…

with prayers like these that show up
sort of pushy, uninvited, and unannounced
one doesn't ask questions

Winter's Work

do you hear that?
his breath at rest
it sounds like dreaming brain
and good tired bones

today he broke up an icy driveway with his new pick
bought at the local hardware store

he brandished it like a weapon,
a diamond.
as I pulled into the driveway,
it blinded me for a second

later baked fragrant perfect dough
tried a new way to put pizza together
veggies beneath, cheese on top
someone asked "how was it"
I said the best I ever I had

It's All Happening at Once

a name or song settles in the psyche
an image or face
appears before your eyes
tattooed on your frontal lobe

thoughts of days gone
or what may come,
where does this chatter
come from?
it all seems too much sometimes

I remember after my mother died
I said out loud to myself
it's like she hasn't left,
but where is she
where did she go

that energy has to have gone
somewhere
and I believed for a while
that she wouldn't completely leave
but instead hover in some seeable reachable realm

she encouraged calm
modeled how to remain present
she had her fears like anyone
but she never cowered

we should sit by a tree and read
allow moments to pass
as if we don't know how to tell time

plant a vigil of rose bushes
don't hesitate to pull them out of the ground
if it becomes clear there will be no roses—merely stay true
and try something new

enrich the soil
choose a fresh bloom

accept everything as a gift
 "don't worry"
  this is what I hear in my head
   from wherever she is, in the far blue

Worry

the vastness takes care of it
I give myself over to resolution
no matter if I meditate or fret
dig a garden or chase dust in sunlight

I accept the small and grand fears
that my imagination uses for good,
as well as reckless
notions of devastation

"it's all normal" …
and what of
this human condition
we call Normal

"you'll lose your parents
your cats
your car keys
me"

yet here I am still,
in and of a world
sleeping quiet,
cocooned within
sky moon stars

rise accept move pulsate sigh open
mustn't let the spoils
have their way
breathe in the delectable possible
expect the universe
to take care of it,
take care of it all

Tiny Plants

most of the women I deeply admire
raise small plants.
cozy prolific communities of
cacti, succulents, and baby ferns
offerings of reassurance

weathered clay pots with matching
drip plates
wiped clean of mites and mold
handmade pottery
earthy, sturdy, aesthetic groupings that complement.
companions who nurture each other in the light and mist

I always look forward to visiting
these human caregivers
my friends
they inspire me to do better
I leave their houses bursting with ideas
that I execute like a happy thief

on my way home
I stop at the garden center
gently place the plants
safe on the floor of my car

carry them into my own forest
tiny growing beings
new grace, more green

Moon Thief

I think everyone has a secret desire to hang out alone
with the moon

our house would grow quiet
little brothers asleep in their beds.
parents cleared away the day's debris
eventually off to their room.
sisters listened to music from a
bedside radio

opportunity presented ...
I'd slip out of bed
to the upstairs bath

in flannel nightgown
I gently maneuvered
the wooden window sash wide open

January's embrace brushed against my face
these were my woods
this was how I took in the night
making sense among the oaks

a sliver of full moon
sliced through branches
reached toward me
as if it understood

The Secret Side of Dorset Street

it's just over the bridge
have you been?

located between dilapidated beauty
and remorse
a graveled road, small surprise
just the kind of place I love

no real views
unless you count the hidden ones
and those 1000 trees

crickets play on repeat
finches never go entirely south
remain behind
amidst fern and dark rich soil

lone cabin
golden autumn
apples, wood smoke, leafy refuse
like frankincense,
blessings upon this revered, decaying cloister

People Watching

idling here alone as late summer
breezes through my passenger window,
I decline your invitation to man-shop.
I am not good with decisions about men's clothes

I don't have the eye.
I can barely dress myself.
some days I play dress-up,
skirts to jeans and back again

but much like the seekers in this parking lot
I long and fret
about age, weight,
sullen partner, hungry children, needy pets

observe styles which range from
refined to raggedy
my brain cannot separate them in this array of
differences, similarities and indecisiveness.

instead, I volunteer to stay behind and take stock
record these comings and goings
note this filling of the mystery void,
however temporary
as they stuff down, soothe
whatever it is I see
etched upon their eager, harrowed faces

The Scent of Hay

aged grass intended as nourishment
fields gone green and gold
against a bottomless lavender sky
while humans toil and sigh

bales rolled and bound
then unfurled,
revelation of layers, little leaves
good and precious clover tucked within
the flavor of this hay
comes our winter in hidden gems

Evening Call

drawn to the porch at dusk
we sit without speaking
until the orchestra begins

wasn't it a vireo we would hear
by the old barn at sunset?
I miss that sound

blue jays' insistent morning squawks.
woke my childhood home
one by one

doves, gold and purple finches
their vibrant tiny bodies
feed, attract, give notice all day long

finally, at evening
the soft trill of shy robins
they, too, sing in daylight
but no one hears them,
drowned out by the din of life
waiting for their chance to say
goodnight again, I love you

Black

the dying come and gone so quickly
though there was no ease;
that concept is a rumor

you'd know what I mean
if you've ever witnessed
tragic immediacy

there there,
he was an animal,
you always knew this day would come

cause of death
blunt force
trauma to the heart

so I practice detachment
acceptance

build a pine box
adorn with thistle
consecrate with sage
(though you laugh and say
he would have hated that)

respect the cairn above
welcoming earth below

grieve for months
isn't that tradition?
it seems so unhealthy, unwieldy

funny how no one notices the wailing widow
grieving mother
perpetual mourner
woman dressed in black

Night Walk

I wish I had a friend
who liked walking in the dark
she would come knock for me at the door,
the way my seventh-grade friends did
when we went to the lake in winter
after I'd washed the dinner dishes
left to dry on their own

snowy sky
skates slung over shoulders
we would make our way to the
frozen lake
the wood fires
the boys

as a young mother
children off to sleep
I and my neighbor friend
(who is long dead)
would meet out on the sidewalk

humidity down
oak leaves at peak growth
perfect measure of
gossip and wisdom

"how to get rid of a sinus headache;
wonder how much the new people paid for their house"

cicadas chirp primal calls
the only other sound,
low timbre of our voices
~~~~~

these days I am satisfied with a brisk, brief neighborly walk
my adventurous friend and I
breathe in the crisp cold night
report on our days, philosophize
(free-form as a child might)
excited talkers, intent listeners.

I notice a woman standing at her kitchen window
washing dishes
lost in thought
lost in the golden light and steam
wishing for stars.

Long Life Rant

if the goal is to achieve very old age
what does that mean
to a woman's essential worth?

is it only a number?
shouldn't quality and charm be deciding factors
in this aging success?

she wants to know
will this old living feel good
will there be friends
lavender lilacs in a vase
yin yoga?

a gold-plated aging trophy
and her own table on which to display this award

she doesn't pray
as old women are known to do
except for her children's
safeness and happiness

and that they will outlive her
of course,
all of which obviously relates to her own happiness
the actual award
sweet selfishness she proudly owns
much like stealing lilacs from
another's late spring garden

Garden People

under an obscured, full moon
children glide onto an icy pond
agile, angelic

awe at the sheer youngness
of such movement and grace
in the night

two people hug closely
on a bench nearby
observe the otherworldly calm
of this insistent moonlight
and the children

"isn't she the library lady?…
he trembles
but it's not because of the cold"

"we know them from the garden,
when it's warm and green," you say,
"where you and I
tend to growing things—
sometimes together."

Wild Bird

birds become strangers
they're leaving now

this morning when I woke
Canada geese flying in V formation
seemingly detached,
as if not a care;

but they do care
for themselves
according to rules of the natural world

watch silent
they rest gently in the field
feed
before lifting off once more
safe warmth
a wild tending

Voice of the Falls

I swing my feet from the wooden bridge
and want to fling a clog off into the rushing below
but what would I do with only one shoe?
  I rethink my desire

Recycled Earth

musical garbage
rustle of plastic bags
some large enough to suffocate a baby seal

a needle lands in the town dump
eventually floats off into an ocean
sometimes dolphins wonder
what the needles taste like.

empty beer bottles after an evening with friends
lined up on a marble countertop,
ready for recycling
instead, the town collects and
buries them in the desert

lush green lawns
simply add a dash of fertilizer
it's the perfect toxic cocktail
may I have a water chaser with that?

so much water
water in my bath
like an ocean
I don't actually bathe, I swim
I swim to the moon

before take-off,
I gather the bags
broken appliances
medical waste
fake palm fronds

for I am the pilot
who promised she would help
I collect all this plastic in a
large, ironic plastic container,
I hope there's room on the moon
in the middle of a crater
on the far side

Day Sense

every day belongs to you
so remember
feed the brain, hug the heart,
go easy on the liver

immerse in the commute,
the flow and calming rhythm of
office, work, food, sleep, family
don't forget nature and music

loyalties and sensibilities matter
whether in a city high rise
a town hall
a country store
or even a dentist's office

calculate math
mix chemicals
write the essay
apply the salve
make history

exercise
save money
listen well
help others
(I mean, really—
isn't it the right thing to do?)
help others help you
show up early
(someone will notice)
take a sick day
breathe

I urge you to
consider problems in the morning
sit at your desk
feign deep thought
press cup of coffee
to forehead

as if you're a magician
preparing to guess which playing card will appear next

when someone passes
and gives you the eye
maybe smile politely
keep a sign nearby that says
"Work in Progress"
leave space for resolution
I promise
you will be saved later, that very same day

Through a Train Window

numbered bridges that span
river and marshlands
offerings of food and shelter
to tern and gull

storm clouds trail behind,
rose purple orange, raging,
speed-gathering past the blue
wrap around dense forest

hot late summer gives way
to northern lights
the gift
in soft rippling undertones

concrete, wasteland, sky, woods
shooting star
return to us
nothing remains the same

Spring Thaw

let it all melt
may it not snow again for 1000 days

I take it all back
what I said last November about cleansings and blessings
I lied

believe me I'm as surprised as you
I should be banished from these mountains for uttering such blasphemy
though this current winter has had its moments.

small children ski their first slope
buses filled with hopeful skiers
on an 'I'm-so-lucky three-day weekend,'
depart with breathy memory of clean air, evergreens
I bet you thought even the booze tasted better.

re-entry to your suburbs and cities will be a total drag
though you're welcome to return.
but me?
I'm done
these past virusy months
I watched snows fall from tedious gray

the things I thought I loved?
woodstove fire
reading books
petting a cat
holing up.
cooking stew.
baking cookies

I never want to taste a winter stew again;
I see no reason for parsnips
I will leave the baking to other women
and practice being a woman in my own way.
honesty
a sigh of relief
shadows trail across my hands
eyes adapt to February sun

Vermont—I abide
but I haven't changed my mind
may it all melt

Jung's Coffee Cup

It is morning once again
time for another night's dream
a flowing universal theme:
enter a house
climb the stairway
descend into a cellar

I interject my usual comments
spiced with Jung
not as if I actually know what I am talking about

but I've taken the standard psych courses
and I read

you say you dreamt of a place
filled with grief and cobwebs
wander aimlessly, questioning
and that I, too, appear in your dream

I say how lucky you are to have recurring dreams
they're like a friend
who is always there for you
even as you sleep

then I realize how lucky am I
to be floating along in these dreams with you
~~~~~
sunlight pours onto our screen porch
my hands hold the coffee's warmth

these early hours are so often the best
as I practice active listening on your behalf;
so go on, tell me more
until your dream is done

Saving

I used to collect sticks at random,
one from Princeton campus when I was 18
I kept it for 40 years until I lost it.
another I found in the woods by my old house

I practically had a breakdown when we left that house
houses are not collectible, nor savable

I saved a tuft of my dead cat's fur
it is tucked inside a small cardboard box in my dresser drawer
I imagined I could summon his DNA from that tuft
and he would return during the night
like an alien visitor

another cat had a heart attack
he died in my arms
it happened so fast
there was no saving him

I stole river stones from Bittersweet Falls
to mark my dead cat's grave

when we moved from the house I loved
I took the stones from his grave
and piled them on a windowsill
in my new house

the stones felt smooth and cool in my hand
as if they'd always belonged to me
and I hadn't stolen them at all

I save photos on my phone.
so many that the Verizon guy rolled his eyes
then he explained how the Cloud could help me with my problem.
I still don't believe him.

I am afraid to lose the photos.
what if I lose the people?
the photos will be all I'd have left
so I hoard the photos and
hope for the best.

my mother and I correspond via U.S. mail
mommy sends me cards from the Immaculate Heart of Mary sisters
I send her artist cards from the co-op
her cards cost $.49 each
mine cost $3.00
both she and I like cards with birds on them
the cost of the birds is irrelevant

I save these cards from my mother;
she is 92 years old
each time one arrives in the mailbox
I think "I am 68 years old
and receive cards from my mother."
I say it out loud for emphasis

her handwriting is Catholic-schoolgirl-holy
my dresser drawer is crammed with these beauties
her beautiful DNA is on them

when she is gone, the cards will make it seem as if she is still with me
like a cat reincarnate
or river stones piled high on a windowsill

While We Wait

they were mysteries apart
as she grieved his demise
the transition from his body was a
somber, listless heartbreak

he would ask for music
accompanied by biblical-grade thrashing
a kiss blown across the room
bye-bye I love you

the end, he handled quietly
a private moment away from the nurse;
stolen from us

but she moved forward
moved boxes of papers that
confirmed her widowhood

eight years without him
until her own time came

she had carried his absence like a handbag
weighted with family photos and shopping lists
this heaviness lived in her throat,
in a dresser stuffed with old sweaters

waited for the man down the hall
who wheeled her to dining
savored delicious chicken soup

returned to her room
chanted Catholic vigils that went nowhere
accomplished little

during that week he lay dying,
I stood behind her as she climbed
the back porch steps into the house
she turned her head, saying
you can't give up
don't ever give up

The Opening

come into my house
sweet people
little ones with stories
I have missed you

strangers no more
time and space reclaimed
we shall grow to know each other better

between politics and pandemic
there has been much
separation
hunger
fear
grief

come to me,
new friend
let us cultivate our novelty with bold humor and new music
forget work and responsibility for a while
make curry
drink deep dark wine
skip school and go hiking in the wild

come back into my life,
dear constant
stream of light and being
always known,
long forgotten
due to mutual misunderstandings
skewed ideals
devious plots
angry fires

I promise you now
hand on my heart
if it convinces you further

come into my house
I will remember kindness
share softness
dispel your fear
feed the hunger
listen to your stories

Eileen Brunetto's writing speaks of cherished solitude and intimate observations of earth and the passage and mystery of time. Her words express hope with a dose of cynicism. As a child growing up in a large family, she walked the nearby woods where she developed a deep appreciation of quiet space—opportunity to think and grow. Trees and the natural environment cultivated curiosity and peace. Her writing laments human disregard of landscape and resources, while reminding us of our need for nature's innate comfort, sustenance, and beauty.

Eileen lives in a central Vermont village with her husband and two cats. She previously lived on "the Ledges" in Cornwall, on a wooded hill, which further cultivated her love of nature and concern for the environment. She worked with Middlebury College's geology department for 20 years, until 2021 in the midst of the pandemic. She is a mother, grandmother, writer, massage therapist, and reiki practitioner. She earned an MFA from Goddard College, Plainfield, Vermont in her 50's while working full time. Her work has been featured in SUNY's *Blueline, Spider Road Press*, and *Zig Zag* literary magazine. She volunteers with a county aging agency, and serves on the Poetry Society of Vermont editorial board. She currently works as a paraeducator at her town elementary school. This is her first poetry chapbook.

www.ingramcontent.com/pod-product-compliance
Lightning Source LLC
Chambersburg PA
CBHW020222090426
42734CB00008B/1177